Cee Cee the CEO

Written by
Aleksandra Malchrzyk

Illustrated by
Magdalena Krupa

Bitsy Tales 2024

This is Cee Cee, a CEO.
Her work is never ever done.

She runs a company and has success.
Does what she always did her best —

Leads and shows people how to ace
Their duties at a really good pace.

Cece inspires and helps to grow
Those whom she hires, don't you know?

She knows what she wants and how to complete
The projects she plans, the deadlines – she meets.

Challenges welcome and overcame.
Cee Cee's nature was never tame.

✓ MBA   ✓ GRADUATE   FLOAT MY COMPANY
✓ START A BUSINESS
✓ ACHIEVE WORK-LIFE BALANCE

She's very tough, sharp, and successful,
And very rarely is she forgetful.

She's well-respected and easy to like,
Because she's fair, just, and alike...

…those who can do rather than not.
Her business plan took just one jot!

She does what she says and has strong will.
A high achiever with excellent skill.

She knows it's not easy to be the boss,
But CEOing is what she loves.

The ceilings she shattered are very many.
She'll swiftly deal with another twenty!

And every girl can be just like Cee Cee
If she decides that's who she'd like to be.

Bitsy Tales

It is a website (www.BitsyTales.com) where a variety of educational and entertaining resources for children and their parents can be found. These include:

"Little Io and the Gem Trail" – a tale that teaches children values such as honesty or perseverance and the meaning behind them. By clicking the 'Customise' button and providing your child(ren)'s name(s), you can make your child(ren) the protagonist(s) of the story, and make it feel special, personal, and even more magical. By using a series of follow-up activities such as quizzes, you can revise the new vocabulary from the story as well as use prompts for discussion and drawing practice.

"Art Smart" – a series of poems designed to teach children about art. It allows children to familiarise themselves with the names of great artists and gives them a little bit of information about each artist's style. It is great for learning about art without leaving the house and encouraging your child's curiosity.

"La, la, tin, tin!" – a poem that introduces children to the beauty and usefulness of the Latin language. It explains where and how Latin is used today and gives ample examples to help teach your child some of the common words and expressions.

The website is being constantly updated so please make sure that you come back every now and then to see what is new!

www.bitsytales.com

About the Authoress

Hello, I am Aleks, the creator of this book.

I have always loved writing and reading. The true inspiration behind what I write is my daughter, Io – I create what I wish to read to her, and then I share it with the wider world. I aim for my writings to be both educational and entertaining. As a former English teacher, I like making sure the learning experience is easy and enjoyable whilst providing a wealth of knowledge and stimulation.

I live in London with my family and whenever I am not buying even more books and reading, I enjoy travelling, doing sports, spending time in nature, eating well, learning, and seeing art.

Sharp Girls Series

Sharp Girls is a series of books written for girls to expose them to inspiring characters and modern perspectives, and give them more courage and confidence in their skills.

One of them is **Mary, a surgeon,** who works at a hospital and saves lives. She is well-educated, ambitious, talented, and determined. Her strength lies in her skills and determination, not the way she looks or tries to fit in.

The board book is written in catchy couplets with rhymes and repetitions children love and teaches them a wealth of new vocabulary. **It is available from the Bitsy Tales shop at BitsyTales.com.**

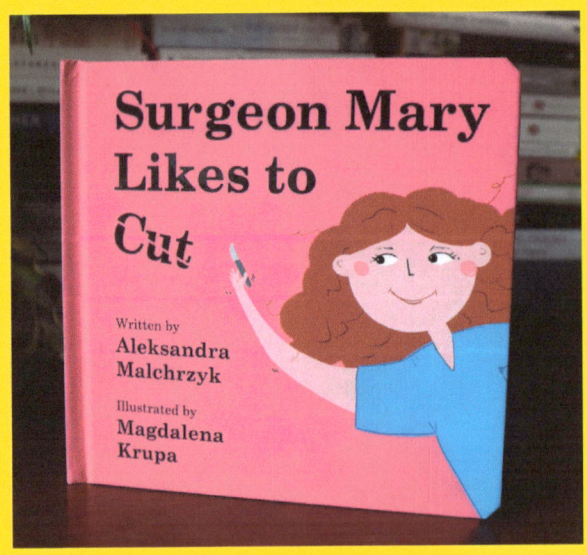

www.ingramcontent.com/pod-product-compliance
Lightning Source LLC
Chambersburg PA
CBHW042129040426
42450CB00002B/124